Table Of Contents

Chapter 1: Understanding Texas Estate Planning Basics

Estate planning and probate avoidance are vital aspects of safeguarding your legacy in the state of Texas. However, it is crucial to understand that the information provided in this book is not intended to serve as legal advice.

The content within this book aims to provide you with a comprehensive guide to Texas estate planning and probate avoidance. It offers valuable insights, tips, and strategies to help you make informed decisions regarding the distribution of your assets, guardianship of your children, and the protection of your loved ones.

It is important to note that laws and regulations related to estate planning and probate may change over time. While every effort has been made to ensure the accuracy and currency of the information provided, it may not reflect the most up-to-date legal or other information available. Therefore, it is advisable to consult with a qualified attorney who specializes in Texas estate planning before making any legal decisions.

Furthermore, it is essential to acknowledge that this book was prepared before the release of any new legislation that may have been enacted by the Texas Legislature in its session in 2023, which will likely become effective in September 2023. Therefore, it may not fully reflect the current legal landscape. Consulting with an attorney will help you navigate any recent changes in the law and ensure your estate plan aligns with the most current regulations.

Remember, estate planning is a complex and individualized process, and the information provided in this book should be used as a general guide and starting point. Your specific circumstances may require unique considerations that can only be addressed by an attorney who can provide tailored advice.

In conclusion, while this book offers valuable insights into Texas estate planning and probate avoidance, it is essential to consult with an attorney for personalized guidance.

Introduction to Estate Planning

Estate planning is a mix of both the rational mind, which knows what to do with the information, and the compassionate mind, which teaches and listens. An estate planning attorney should never lose sight of these principles. Your attorney should spend the time necessary to truly understand your goals and objectives. How you and your attorney plan your estate will have a profound impact on your families and the ones you love. As a client, you have the right to expect your attorney to strive to help you identify your greatest hopes, fears, dreams, and aspirations.

Estate planning is a crucial aspect of ensuring the financial security and well-being of your loved ones after your passing. It involves making important decisions about the distribution of your assets, the care of your children, and the management of your affairs. In this subchapter, we will provide you with an overview of estate planning and its significance in the context of Texas law.

You have undoubtedly worked hard to build a life for your family, accumulating assets along the way. Estate planning allows you to protect and preserve these assets, ensuring they are passed on according to your wishes. It also provides a framework for addressing potential complications that may arise during the distribution of your estate.

Specifically tailored to Texas, this book aims to guide you through the intricacies of estate planning and probate avoidance. Texas estate planning laws have their own unique characteristics that may differ from those in other states. Therefore, it is essential to gain a comprehensive understanding of the legal framework specific to Texas to make informed decisions about your estate.

By delving into the chapters of this book, you will learn about the various tools and strategies available to effectively plan your estate. From wills and trusts to powers of attorney and healthcare directives, we will explore the different instruments that can help protect your assets, minimize taxes, and ensure your family's financial stability.

Moreover, we will address the importance of probate avoidance in estate planning. Probate is the legal process through which a deceased person's assets are distributed and their debts are settled. While it is a necessary procedure, it can be time-consuming, expensive, and potentially contentious. We will provide insights into how you can structure your estate plan to minimize or avoid the probate process altogether.

Understanding the nuances of estate planning is crucial for Texans, as it serves as a safeguard for their future. By taking the time to educate yourself about Texas estate planning laws and exploring different strategies, you can secure your legacy and provide your loved ones with financial stability and peace of mind.

Importance of Estate Planning for Texas Residents

When it comes to planning for the future, there is no better time than now. As adults with children, we have a responsibility to ensure the financial security and well-being of our loved ones, even after we are no longer here. Estate planning plays a vital role in achieving this goal, providing a comprehensive roadmap for the distribution of assets and the protection of our legacy.

One of the primary reasons estate planning is essential for Texas residents is the avoidance of probate. Probate is the legal process through which a deceased person's assets are distributed and debts are settled. While probate can be a lengthy and expensive process, proper estate planning allows you to bypass it altogether. By utilizing tools such as revocable living trusts, Texas residents can transfer assets directly to their beneficiaries, avoiding the need for probate court involvement.

Additionally, estate planning allows you to protect your children's financial future. Through the creation of a comprehensive will, you can designate guardianship for your minor children, ensuring they are cared for by someone you trust in the event of your untimely passing. Estate planning also allows you to establish a trust for your children, protecting their inheritance from mismanagement or potential creditors.

Moreover, estate planning goes beyond the distribution of assets. It also encompasses healthcare directives, such as living wills and powers of attorney. These documents allow you to make important medical decisions on behalf of yourself or your loved ones, ensuring that your wishes are respected in critical situations.

In "Secure Your Legacy: A Comprehensive Guide to Texas Estate Planning," I provide you with the necessary tools and knowledge to navigate the complexities of estate planning in Texas. Whether you are just starting your estate planning journey or need to update your existing plan, this book serves as a valuable resource for Texas residents seeking to secure their legacy and protect their loved ones.

Don't leave your family's financial future to chance. Take control of your estate planning today and ensure that your assets are distributed according to your wishes, while minimizing the burdens of probate. Secure Your Legacy is your guide to achieving peace of mind and leaving a lasting impact on future generations.

Key Terms and Concepts in Estate Planning

Estate planning is a crucial process that every adult with children should consider. It involves making important decisions about how your assets will be managed and distributed after your passing. To help you navigate through the complex world of Texas estate planning and probate avoidance, this subchapter will familiarize you with key terms and concepts essential to understanding the process.

1. Last Will and Testament: This legal document outlines your wishes regarding the distribution of your assets, appoints guardians for minor children, and names an executor to oversee the administration of your estate.

2. Trust: A trust is a legal arrangement that allows a third party, known as a trustee, to hold and manage assets on behalf of beneficiaries. Trusts can be revocable or irrevocable and offer various benefits, such as avoiding probate and providing for minor children or individuals with special needs.

3. Probate: Probate is the legal process through which a court validates a will, settles debts, and distributes assets. Understanding probate avoidance strategies, such as creating a living trust, can save your loved one's time and money.

4. Power of Attorney: A power of attorney is a legal document that grants someone else the authority to make financial or healthcare decisions on your behalf if you become incapacitated.

5. Guardianship: Naming a guardian for your minor children is crucial in estate planning. By designating a trusted individual to care for your children, you ensure they will be raised according to your values and wishes.

6. Estate Tax: Estate tax is a tax imposed on the transfer of assets after death. Understanding the current estate tax laws and utilizing appropriate strategies can help minimize the tax burden on your estate.

7. Beneficiary Designations: Certain assets, such as life insurance policies and retirement accounts, allow you to name beneficiaries directly. Ensuring your beneficiary designations are up to date is essential for proper estate planning.

8. Medicaid Planning: Medicaid is a government program that provides long-term care assistance. Engaging in Medicaid planning can help protect your assets while still qualifying for Medicaid benefits if needed in the future.

By familiarizing yourself with these key terms and concepts, you will be better equipped to make informed decisions about your Texas estate planning and probate avoidance strategies. Remember, estate planning is not a one-time event but an ongoing process that should be reviewed periodically to ensure it reflects your current circumstances and goals.

Consulting with an experienced estate planning attorney can provide invaluable guidance tailored to your specific needs. Secure Your Legacy: A Comprehensive Guide to Texas Estate Planning offers further insights and practical advice to help you protect your assets, provide for your loved ones, and leave a lasting legacy.

Common Misconceptions about Estate Planning in Texas

When it comes to estate planning, there are several common misconceptions that many adults with children in Texas have. These misconceptions can often lead to costly mistakes or missed opportunities to protect and secure your legacy. In this subchapter, we will debunk these misconceptions and provide you with the right information to make informed decisions about your estate planning.

Misconception 1: "I have a Will so I won't go through probate." Countless people I have talked with interacted with online regarding one of my video presentations say they were shocked to discover that their Will has no legal effect until a probate judge has deemed it meets the statutory requirements for Texas and is deemed valid. They thought they could just carry the Will into the bank after their loved one passed and they would have access. I think for me that is the most surprising misconception I have seen. I was probably the same before law school decades ago and most people rarely deal with attorneys or probate so the misconception continue.

Misconception 2: "I don't need estate planning because I don't have a large estate."
Many people believe that estate planning is only necessary for those with substantial wealth. However, estate planning is not solely about wealth distribution. It encompasses various aspects such as guardianship for minor children, healthcare directives, and even pet care arrangements. Regardless of your net worth, estate planning ensures that your wishes are followed, and your loved ones are protected.

Misconception 3: "I have a will, so I don't need any additional estate planning documents."
While a will is an essential part of estate planning, it is not the only document you need. Other crucial documents include an up-to-date durable power of attorney, healthcare power of attorney, and living will. These documents provide instructions for financial and healthcare decisions in case you become incapacitated. Without

them, your loved ones may face challenges and legal hurdles during difficult times.

Misconception 4: "I can do my estate planning on my own."
While it may be tempting to create your estate plan using online templates or DIY kits, it can be risky. Estate planning is a complex legal process that requires expertise and knowledge of state laws. Working with an experienced estate planning attorney ensures that your plan is tailored to your specific needs, complies with Texas laws, and avoids common pitfalls. Sorry to say this, but you will only know if your plan worked once you're dead. Therefore, when comparing the minimal amount you will spend in preparing an Estate Plan compare that to the value of your Estate. You could easily have $500,000 tied up in a fairly reasonable home here in Texas, then add various other accounts and assets and few thousands dollars spent now on helping your family avoid probate is actually an investment because there is a return on the money paid for estate planning.

Misconception 5: "My estate won't go through probate, so I don't need to worry about it."
Probate is the legal process of distributing a deceased person's estate. Many people believe that their estate will automatically avoid probate, but this is not always the case. Without proper planning, your estate may still go through probate, which can be time-consuming and expensive. In Texas if you own a home there are a couple tools we use to avoid probate, but if you don't use on then that home will cause your family to go through probate. Exploring probate avoidance strategies, such as trusts, Transfer on Death Deeds, etc. can help simplify the process and preserve your assets for your beneficiaries.

By understanding and debunking these misconceptions, you can make informed decisions about your estate planning. Consulting with an estate planning attorney who specializes in Texas laws is the best way to ensure that your plan is comprehensive, legally sound, and reflects your unique circumstances and goals. Remember, estate planning is not just for the wealthy; it is for everyone who wants to protect their loved ones and secure their legacy.

Taking Stock of Your Assets and Liabilities

One of the initial steps in securing your legacy is to take stock of your assets and liabilities. This subchapter will guide you through the process, ensuring that you have a comprehensive understanding of your financial situation.

First and foremost, it is essential to gather all the necessary documentation. This includes financial statements, property deeds, investment portfolios, retirement account statements, life insurance policies, and any other relevant documents. By organizing these documents, you will have a clear overview of your assets and liabilities.

Once you have collected the necessary paperwork, it is time to assess your assets. Consider all your tangible and intangible possessions, including real estate, vehicles, valuable collectibles, bank accounts, stocks, bonds, and business interests. Assign each asset a value and categorize them accordingly. This process will enable you to determine the overall worth of your estate.

While assessing your assets, it is equally important to evaluate your liabilities. This includes mortgages, loans, credit card debts, and any other outstanding financial obligations. By understanding your liabilities, you can make informed decisions regarding your estate planning, such as ensuring that your loved ones are not burdened with debt after your passing.

Once you have a clear picture of your assets and liabilities, it is time to consider your goals and desires for your estate. Do you want to leave a specific amount of money to each of your children? Are there any charitable organizations you wish to support? By setting clear objectives, you can tailor your estate plan accordingly, ensuring that your wishes are fulfilled.

Additionally, taking stock of your assets and liabilities allows you to identify potential gaps in your estate plan. Are there any assets that have not been properly accounted for? Are there any beneficiaries or heirs that you have not named? By identifying these gaps, you can work with an estate planning attorney to create a comprehensive plan that addresses all your concerns.

I will add that the more you go about placing all of these documents in one place and updating the documents routinely the easier it will be on your family. Countless families are almost in shock after their loved one dies and then they discover that they have to go on a treasure hunt just to locate all of these important documents related to your assets. Do them a favor and put them in a specific place preferably in a fireproof box and tell them if something happens that is where you will find all of my key documents along with your estate plan documents.

Understanding the Value of Your Estate

It is important to have a comprehensive understanding of the value of your estate. This knowledge plays a vital role in Texas estate planning and probate avoidance. By understanding the value of your estate, you can make informed decisions about how to protect and distribute your assets, ensuring a secure legacy for your loved ones.

The value of your estate includes all your assets, such as real estate, investments, retirement accounts, life insurance policies, and personal belongings. It is crucial to have an accurate assessment of these assets to effectively plan for the future. Valuing your estate can be a complex process, and seeking professional assistance from an estate planning attorney is highly recommended.

One aspect of estate valuation is determining the fair market value of your assets. This involves assessing the current worth of your property, taking into consideration factors such as market conditions and depreciation. An experienced attorney can guide you through this process, ensuring that your assets are accurately valued.

Knowing the value of your estate enables you to explore various strategies for probate avoidance, such as establishing a living trust. A living trust allows you to transfer your assets into a trust during your lifetime, bypassing the need for probate. This not only ensures a smoother transfer of assets but also maintains privacy and reduces administrative costs.

Additionally, understanding the value of your estate helps you make informed decisions regarding taxes. Estate taxes can significantly reduce the value of your assets passed on to your loved ones. By working with an estate planning attorney, you can explore various strategies to minimize estate taxes, such as gifting, charitable donations, or establishing trusts.

In conclusion, understanding the value of your estate is crucial in Texas estate planning and probate avoidance. By accurately assessing the worth of your assets, you can make informed decisions about protecting and distributing your estate. Seeking professional guidance from an estate planning attorney is highly recommended to ensure that your legacy is secure and your loved ones are provided for.

Identifying Your Beneficiaries and Heirs

One of the most crucial steps in estate planning is identifying your beneficiaries and heirs.

When it comes to estate planning, identifying beneficiaries and heirs is not a task to be taken lightly. It involves making decisions about who will inherit your assets, property, and finances. Without proper planning, the distribution of your estate may become subject to legal battles, delays, and unnecessary expenses. By clearly identifying your beneficiaries and heirs, you can avoid such complications and provide for your loved ones according to your wishes.

Estate planning and probate avoidance hold particular significance due to the state's unique laws and regulations. Understanding these intricacies is crucial to ensure that your assets are protected and distributed efficiently. By consulting with an experienced estate planning attorney who specializes in Texas law, you can navigate through the complexities of the process and optimize your plan accordingly.

When identifying your beneficiaries, consider not only your immediate family but also any other individuals or organizations you wish to include. It is essential to carefully outline and update your beneficiaries in your estate planning documents, such as your will, trust, or any other instruments you may have in place. By doing so, you can provide clarity and minimize potential conflicts among your heirs.

Additionally, it is crucial to review and update your beneficiaries regularly, especially during significant life events such as marriages, divorces, births, or deaths. Failing to update your beneficiaries can result in unintended consequences, such as leaving assets to ex-spouses or excluding new family members.

In conclusion, identifying your beneficiaries and heirs is a vital step in estate planning, particularly for adults with children. By taking the time to carefully consider and update your beneficiaries, you can ensure that your legacy is secure and that your loved ones are provided for after you're gone.

Evaluating Special Considerations for Minor Children

If you have minor children, ensuring the well-being and protection of your children should be at the forefront of your planning process. This subchapter will delve into the special considerations that parents in Texas need to address when creating their estate plans.

One of the most important aspects to consider is selecting a guardian for your children. This decision should be made after careful thought and discussion with potential candidates. Your chosen guardian should be someone you trust implicitly, who understands your values, and who is willing and able to assume the responsibility of raising your children in the event of your untimely passing.

Financial considerations are equally important. Establishing a trust for your children can help ensure their financial stability even after you are no longer there to provide for them. Through a trust, you can designate a trustee who will manage the assets on behalf of your minor children until they reach a certain age or milestone, such as completing higher education. This provides a level of protection and oversight to ensure that your children's inheritance is managed responsibly.

In Texas, it is essential to be aware of the Uniform Transfers to Minors Act (UTMA). This act allows you to transfer assets to your minor children without the need for a trust. However, it is crucial to understand the potential drawbacks and limitations of this approach, such as the lack of control over how the assets are used once the child reaches the age of majority.

Additionally, considering the potential impact of estate taxes on your children's inheritance is vital. Texas does not have a state estate tax, but federal estate tax laws may still apply. Working with an experienced estate planning attorney can help you navigate these complexities and implement strategies to minimize or eliminate estate taxes, ensuring that more of your assets pass on to your children.

Lastly, regularly reviewing and updating your estate plan is crucial, especially as your children grow and their needs change. Revisit your plan after significant life events, such as the birth of additional children, divorce, or remarriage, to ensure that your wishes align with your current circumstances.

By evaluating these special considerations for minor children in your estate plan, you can have peace of mind knowing that you have taken the necessary steps to secure your children's future and protect their well-being.

Chapter 3: Creating a Will in Texas

Understanding the Role and Purpose of a Will

In the realm of Texas estate planning one crucial document that every adult should be familiar with is a will. A will serves as a vital tool in ensuring that your final wishes are carried out and your loved ones are provided for after your passing. This subchapter aims to shed light on the role and purpose of a will, empowering you to make informed decisions when it comes to securing your legacy.

Most people who seek the will services of a lawyer look to him or her for guidance. When asked by a lawyer what they want to do in their wills, they often reply, "Leave everything to my spouse, and then to my children equally." The result is almost always a simple paragraph or two saying just that (with a little Latin thrown in) and nothing more. The rest of the will document (and most trusts for that matter) is bare-bones boilerplate: sterile legalese that does not have any loving instructions for the care of spouses, children, and grandchildren. Software wills are perhaps the worst choice because many are either invalid or grossly ineffective because people have no real idea as to the legal impact of the selections they make.

First and foremost, a will is a legal document that allows you to dictate how your assets will be distributed upon your death. It provides you with the autonomy to designate beneficiaries and specify the portion of your estate they will receive. By clearly outlining your wishes, you can minimize confusion, disagreements, and potential conflicts among family members, ensuring your intentions are carried out smoothly.

Additionally, a will allows you to nominate a guardian for your minor children, should both parents pass away. This provision is of utmost importance, as it ensures your children will be cared for by someone you trust and who shares your values. By naming a guardian in your will, you can provide peace of mind and stability for your children during a challenging time.

Furthermore, a will allows you to select an executor who will be responsible for managing your estate and ensuring your wishes are fulfilled. This individual will handle tasks such as gathering and distributing assets, paying debts, and navigating the probate process. Choosing a competent and trustworthy executor is crucial, as they will play a vital role in the efficient administration of your estate.

It is important to note that without a valid will in place, your estate will be subject to intestate succession laws. This means that the distribution of your assets will be determined by state law, which may not align with your wishes or adequately provide for your loved ones. By crafting a will, you can take control of your estate planning and shape your legacy according to your values and desires.

If you die without a will, intestate, then as mentioned the rules of descent and distribution as setup in the Texas Estates Code will determine who receives your property. Not only is a will a good start it allows you to determine who receives your property and will save you $750-$1,250. If you die without a will and your estate goes through probate the judge is required to appoint an attorney ad litem to investigate the application and confirm it contains all the decedent's known heirs. The attorney ad litem will typically call people named in the application, look at genealogy sites in an attempt to thoroughly confirm for the court that are heirs have been named.

In conclusion, a will is a powerful tool used for estate planning and probate avoidance. It allows you to dictate the distribution of your assets, appoint a guardian for your children, and select an executor to manage your estate. By understanding the role and purpose of a will, you can make informed decisions that secure your legacy and provide for your loved ones in the future.

Drafting Your Will: Essential Components and Considerations

As adults proactively planning your legacy, you understand the importance of planning for the future and ensuring that your loved ones are taken care of when you are no longer around. One crucial aspect of securing your legacy is drafting a will that outlines your wishes and distributes your assets in the way you desire. In this subchapter, we will explore the essential components and considerations of drafting a will specifically tailored to minimize the impact of probate on your estate through careful planning.

First and foremost, a will should clearly state your intentions regarding the distribution of your assets. It should include a list of your beneficiaries, whether they are family members, friends, or charitable organizations, and specify the portion of the estate each will receive. It is essential to update your will regularly as circumstances change, such as births, deaths, or changes in your relationships.

Furthermore, your will should appoint an executor, someone you trust to carry out your wishes and handle the administrative tasks involved in settling your estate. The executor will be responsible for paying any outstanding debts, and taxes, and distributing assets according to your instructions. Naming a backup executor is also advisable in case the primary one is unable or unwilling to fulfill their duties.

Considerations for estate planning and probate avoidance include the use of trusts. Trusts can be beneficial for protecting assets, minimizing estate taxes, and avoiding probate. They can also be used to provide for minor children or loved ones with special needs. Understanding the different types of trusts available and how they align with your goals is crucial when drafting your will.

Additionally, it is essential to consider guardianship for your minor children. Designating a guardian in your will ensures that your children will be cared for by someone you trust and who shares your values. Discussing this responsibility with potential guardians beforehand is recommended to ensure their willingness and ability to assume this role.

Lastly, it is wise to consult with an experienced estate planning attorney who specializes in Texas law. They can guide you through the complex process, help you avoid common pitfalls, and ensure that your will is legally sound.

In conclusion, drafting a will is a vital first step in securing your legacy and providing for your loved ones. By including essential components such as asset distribution, designation of an executor, consideration of trusts, and guardianship for minor children, you can ensure that your wishes are carried out and your family is protected. With the assistance of a knowledgeable estate planning attorney, you can navigate the intricacies of Texas estate planning and probate avoidance, ensuring a smooth transition for your loved ones when the time comes.

Choosing an Executor for Your Will

One of the most important decisions you will make when creating your estate plan is selecting an executor for your will. The executor is responsible for carrying out your final wishes and ensuring that your estate is distributed according to your instructions. This role requires someone who is trustworthy, organized, and capable of handling the complex tasks involved in settling an estate.

When choosing an executor, it is crucial to consider the unique circumstances of your family and the specific requirements of Texas estate planning and probate avoidance. Here are some factors to consider:

1. Trustworthiness: The executor will have access to your financial accounts, assets, and personal information. It is essential to choose someone you trust implicitly to handle these matters with integrity and honesty.

2. Organizational skills: Settling an estate can be a complex process involving paperwork, legal filings, and communication with banks, creditors, and beneficiaries. An executor should be detail-oriented and capable of managing these tasks efficiently.

3. Availability: Being an executor requires a significant time commitment. Choose someone who has the time and availability to dedicate to the role, as settling an estate can take months or even years.

4. Financial knowledge: While not necessary, having an executor with a basic understanding of financial matters can be advantageous. They will be responsible for managing and distributing your assets, paying any outstanding debts, and handling tax filings.

5. Family dynamics: Consider the relationships between potential executors and your beneficiaries. If there are potential conflicts or tensions, it may be wise to choose an executor who can remain impartial and navigate these complexities.

6. Professional expertise: In some cases, it may be beneficial to choose an attorney, accountant, or financial advisor as your executor. Their professional knowledge can be invaluable in navigating the legal and financial aspects of estate planning and probate avoidance. Do note that this will typically be the most expensive option, but for some people that is the only option.

Remember, you can choose more than one executor. Co-executors can work together to share the responsibilities and provide a checks-and-balances system. I generally advise against naming Co-anything simply because as you would guess if no one is the one in charge sometimes no decisions will get made and it can simply cause unneeded drama at the last time a family needs to face it right after the death of a loved one.

Once you have chosen an executor, it is essential to have an open and honest conversation with them about your expectations and the responsibilities involved. Make sure they are willing to take on the role and understand the complexity of the task.

Choosing an executor for your will is a crucial decision that should not be taken lightly. By considering the specific requirements of Texas estate planning and probate avoidance, as well as the unique dynamics of your family, you can ensure that your final wishes are carried out effectively and efficiently.

Updating and Maintaining Your Will

As life evolves, so do your circumstances and priorities. Therefore, it is crucial to regularly review and update your will to ensure that it accurately reflects your wishes and protects your loved ones. In this subchapter, we will delve into the importance of updating and maintaining your will, specifically tailored to Texas estate planning and probate avoidance.

Firstly, let us emphasize the significance of reviewing your will after major life events. Whether you have recently married, divorced, had children, or experienced the loss of a loved one, these events can have a significant impact on your estate planning. By promptly updating your will, you can ensure that your assets are distributed according to your current wishes and that your children are adequately provided for.

In Texas, there are specific laws and regulations that govern estate planning and probate, making it crucial to stay informed about any changes. By regularly consulting with an experienced estate planning attorney, you can stay up-to-date on the latest legal developments and ensure that your will complies with all the necessary requirements. This step is particularly important if you have recently moved to Texas or own property in multiple states.

It is also essential to consider the impact of changing tax laws on your estate plan. Tax laws are subject to frequent revisions, and understanding how these changes can affect your assets is crucial for effective estate planning. By working with a knowledgeable attorney, you can assess the potential tax implications and make any necessary adjustments to your will to minimize tax burdens for your beneficiaries.

Lastly, regular maintenance of your will is essential to keep it accurate and relevant. We recommend reviewing your will at least every three to five years, or whenever a significant life event occurs. In addition to reviewing your will, it is essential to keep your financial and personal records organized and easily accessible. This will facilitate the administration of your estate and ensure that your loved ones can easily locate and access important documents when needed.

In conclusion, updating and maintaining your will is a vital aspect of Texas estate planning and probate avoidance. By staying proactive, regularly reviewing your will, and seeking professional guidance, you can ensure that your estate plan accurately reflects your wishes and effectively protects your loved ones. Remember, a well-maintained will provides peace of mind, knowing that your legacy is secure and your loved ones' future is protected.

Introduction to Trusts and Their Benefits

One powerful tool that can help achieve these goals is the use of trusts in estate planning. In this subchapter, we will explore the concept of trusts and the numerous benefits they offer, specifically within the context of Texas estate planning and probate avoidance.

A trust is a legal entity that allows you to transfer assets, such as property, money, or investments, to a designated trustee who will manage and distribute these assets according to your wishes. By establishing a trust, you gain greater control over your assets and can ensure that they are used for the intended purposes.

One significant benefit of using trusts in Texas estate planning is the ability to avoid probate. By placing your assets in a trust, you can bypass the probate process, saving your family from unnecessary stress and potential conflicts.

Moreover, trusts offer enhanced privacy compared to wills. Unlike wills, trusts are not subject to public records, meaning that the details of your estate plan will remain confidential. This aspect is particularly important in Texas, where public probate records can be easily accessed by anyone.

Another advantage of trusts is their flexibility. They can be tailored to suit your specific needs and goals. For instance, if you have minor children, you can establish a trust that designates a guardian and outlines the management of their inheritance until they reach a certain age or achieve specific milestones. Trusts allow you to protect your children's financial future while ensuring that they are provided for in the best possible way. A Trust can also be used to protect adult children who don't manage money well or might be subject to a lawsuit or bankruptcy as protection can be inserted to just pay out an allowance monthly. Similarly, your Trust can have language providing that the trustee cease all payments to a drug-addicted child except for rehabilitation, and after rehabilitation the trustee can request a drug test monthly to continue making payments for one year after release from rehab.

In addition, trusts can also be used to minimize estate taxes, protect assets from creditors, and even support charitable causes. These versatile tools provide a wide range of options to meet your unique circumstances and desires.

In this subchapter, we will delve deeper into the different types of trusts available, explain the process of establishing and managing a trust, and highlight specific considerations relevant to Texas residents. By understanding the ins and outs of trusts, you can make informed decisions that will safeguard your legacy and provide for your family's well-being.

Remember, estate planning is not just about securing your own future but also about ensuring financial security and peace of mind for those you leave behind. Trusts can play a vital role in achieving these objectives, and this subchapter will equip you with the necessary knowledge to make the most of this powerful estate planning tool.

Exploring Different Types of Trusts

In the world of estate planning and probate avoidance, trusts play a crucial role in securing and preserving your legacy. Understanding the different types of trusts available to you is essential in making informed decisions regarding the distribution of your assets and the protection of your loved ones. This subchapter delves into the various types of trusts commonly used in Texas, giving you a comprehensive overview of their features and benefits.

Revocable Living Trusts: As the most popular type of trust, revocable living trusts offer flexibility and control. They allow you to maintain ownership and control over your assets during your lifetime while designating beneficiaries who will receive them upon your passing or choosing to have your assets held in trust by your successor trustee until a certain age or milestone has been accomplished by your children. I was recently informed of the passing of one of my past clients. He had set his trust up to distribute everything upon his death. Even though his children were in their late 20's he was not concerned. After a recent talk with his financial planner, he said after client's death a few years ago the kids had almost spent his entire estate in a matter of a few years with one ending up in jail. These are the hard truths I tell clients is we don't know what the future holds and dropping $1M or even $500K into your child's lap may inadvertently diminish their desire to have a strong work ethic, fail to learn to save money, or just become totally dependent on trust funds and never accomplish anything. I generally suggest that a child receive nothing except what is needed for their health safety and welfare until later in life. The client has to choose an age so perhaps that is 45 years old. It can be set to distribute a third at 25, another third at 35 and the balance at age 45. These ages are totally up to the client and the family dynamics, but it is just another area where dealing with a professional can add value to help you avoid certain pitfalls i have seen or that have been shared with me. Additionally, revocable living trusts can help you avoid probate, and ensure a smooth transfer of your assets to your loved ones.

Irrevocable Life Insurance Trusts: Life insurance is a vital component of any estate plan, but it can have tax implications if not structured correctly. An irrevocable life insurance trust is designed to hold your life insurance policies, removing them from your taxable estate and potentially reducing your estate tax liability. This trust ensures that the proceeds from your life insurance policy are distributed to your beneficiaries efficiently and without unnecessary tax burdens.

Supplemental Needs Trusts: If you have a loved one with special needs, a supplemental needs trust provides a means to support them financially without interfering with their eligibility for government benefits. This trust can be used to manage their assets and provide for their care, granting you peace of mind knowing that their needs will be met even after you are gone.

Charitable Remainder Trusts: For those with a philanthropic spirit, charitable remainder trusts allow you to leave a lasting impact on the causes you care about. By transferring assets into this trust, you can receive income from the trust during your lifetime while ensuring that the remaining assets are donated to a charity of your choice upon your passing. This type of trust allows you to support charitable organizations while potentially enjoying tax benefits.

Pet Trusts: Texas does legally allow you to set up a pet trust that will be designed to provide financial resources to take care of your pet along with naming a Trustee and a person who will oversee the finances and care of your pet(s)

Understanding the different types of trusts available in Texas enables you to create a comprehensive and personalized plan that meets your specific needs and goals. By consulting with an experienced estate planning attorney, you can navigate the intricacies of these trusts and design an estate plan that secures your legacy and ensures the financial well-being of your loved ones.

Establishing and Funding a Trust

. In this subchapter, we will delve into the essential aspects of establishing and funding a trust, focusing on Texas estate planning and probate avoidance.

A trust is a legal entity that allows you to transfer assets to a trustee, who will manage and distribute them according to your instructions. By creating a trust, you gain greater control over how your assets are utilized and distributed, even after your passing. This ensures that your children are provided for, and your wishes are respected.

To establish a trust, you need to identify your goals and select the type of trust that best aligns with your objectives. In Texas, popular types of trusts include revocable living trusts, special needs trusts, and testamentary trusts. Each has its own advantages and considerations, so it is crucial to consult with an experienced estate planning attorney to determine the most suitable option for your specific circumstances.

Once you have established a trust, funding the trust becomes essential. This involves transferring assets into the trust's ownership. Funding can be done through various means, such as retitling assets, changing beneficiary designations, or assigning ownership interests.

By funding your trust, you ensure that the assets are protected and can be efficiently managed by the trustee.

This is a step that some overlook and then the trust is just a nice-looking document that actually accomplished nothing. I have encountered clients who had a plan prepared by an attorney and perhaps he advised them to fund the trust, but it never was accomplished. When I prepare a plan that includes a trust I always handle conveying real estate into the trust by simply preparing a deed where the client deeds the home to the client's revocable living trust and confirm it gets recorded with the appropriate county. Then in addition, part of our planning is to determine what current accounts they have that we will move into an account titled in the name of the trust. Do note that we do not ordinarily try to change title to any qualified accounts this would include an IRA, 401(k), 403(b), etc.

By establishing and funding a trust, you can effectively avoid probate, ensuring a smoother transfer of your assets to your beneficiaries.

However, it is essential to note that establishing and funding a trust is not a one-time task. Regular review and updating of your trust are crucial to ensure it reflects your current wishes and circumstances. Life events such as marriage, birth, divorce, or changes in financial situations may necessitate modifications to your trust.

By creating a trust, you gain control over the distribution of your assets, ensuring your children's well-being and securing your legacy. Consult with an experienced estate planning attorney to establish a trust that aligns with your goals and regularly review and update it to reflect changes in your life. With a well-structured trust in place, you can have peace of mind knowing that your loved ones will be provided for in the future.

Administering and Managing a Trust

Once you have established a trust as part of your estate planning strategy, it is crucial to understand how to effectively administer and manage it. Administering a trust involves carrying out the wishes and instructions of the trust creator, ensuring that assets are distributed according to their wishes, and managing the trust's ongoing affairs. This subchapter will guide you through the essential aspects of administering and managing a trust, providing you with the knowledge and tools necessary to secure your legacy.

One of the first steps in administering a trust is identifying and understanding your role as a trustee. As a trustee, you have a fiduciary duty to act in the best interest of the trust's beneficiaries. This includes managing and protecting the trust assets, making prudent investment decisions, and ensuring the beneficiaries receive their distributions as outlined in the trust document.

Proper record-keeping is paramount when administering a trust. You will need to keep detailed records of all trust transactions, including investments, expenses, and distributions. This not only helps you fulfill your duty as a trustee but can also be invaluable in case of any disputes or legal challenges that may arise.

Communication with beneficiaries is another crucial aspect of trust administration. Regularly updating beneficiaries about the trust's progress, addressing any concerns or questions they may have, and ensuring transparency can help foster a positive relationship and minimize misunderstandings.

As a trustee, you may also need to work closely with professionals such as attorneys, accountants, and financial advisors. These experts can provide guidance on legal and financial matters, help you navigate complex tax laws, and ensure that the trust's assets are properly managed and protected.

Throughout the administration process, it is essential to stay informed about any changes in trust laws and regulations. Estate planning and trust laws can evolve, and staying up-to-date will help you make informed decisions and maintain compliance with the law.

By effectively administering and managing a trust, you can ensure that your assets are protected, your beneficiaries are provided for, and your legacy is preserved. This subchapter will equip you with the necessary knowledge and practical tips to navigate the complexities of trust administration, ensuring a smooth and successful implementation of your Texas estate planning strategy.

Remember, securing your legacy goes beyond creating a trust; it also involves actively managing and protecting it for the benefit of future generations.

Chapter 5: Power of Attorney and Medical Power of Attorney and Advanced Healthcare Directives

Chapter 5: Power of Attorney and Medical Power of Attorney and Advanced Healthcare Directives

When it comes to estate planning in Texas, it is crucial for adults with children to understand the significance of powers of attorney and advanced healthcare directives. In this chapter, we will explore how these legal documents can help secure your legacy and ensure your wishes are respected.

1. Understanding Powers of Attorney:
A power of attorney is a legal document that grants someone else the authority to act on your behalf in financial and legal matters. By designating a trusted individual as your agent, you can ensure that your affairs will be managed if you become incapacitated or are unable to make decisions. We will delve into the various types of powers of attorney available in Texas and discuss the importance of choosing the right agent.

2. Medical Power of Attorney:
A medical power of attorney allows you to appoint someone as your healthcare agent, empowering them to make medical decisions on your behalf if you are unable to do so. We will discuss the importance of selecting a healthcare agent who understands your values and preferences. This document ensures that your medical

treatment aligns with your wishes, providing peace of mind for both you and your loved ones.

3. Advanced Healthcare Directives:
Advanced healthcare directives, such as living wills and do-not-resuscitate orders, give you control over your medical treatment in specific situations. We will explore the benefits of having these directives in place and discuss how they work in conjunction with a medical power of attorney. By clearly expressing your healthcare preferences, you can relieve your family of the burden of making difficult decisions on your behalf.

Throughout this chapter, we will emphasize the importance of discussing these matters with your family and loved ones. By openly communicating your wishes, you can avoid potential conflicts and ensure that everyone is on the same page regarding your medical and financial decisions.

Additionally, we will address the specific laws and regulations surrounding powers of attorney and advanced healthcare directives in Texas. Understanding the legal requirements will help you create valid and enforceable documents that provide the maximum protection for you and your family.

Remember, estate planning is not just about protecting your assets; it is about securing your legacy and ensuring your loved ones are taken care of. By harnessing the power of attorney and advanced healthcare directives, you can have peace of mind knowing that your wishes will be respected in the face of any unforeseen circumstances.

Understanding the Importance of a Statutory Durable Power of Attorney

When it comes to Estate Planning one crucial aspect that one must understand is the importance of a Statutory Durable Power of Attorney (hereafter "Power of Attorney"). This legal document grants someone the authority to act on your behalf in financial, legal, and other financial matters if you become incapacitated or are unable to make decisions for yourself. It is a vital tool in ensuring that your wishes are carried out and your loved ones are protected.

In the event of an unexpected accident or illness, having a Power of Attorney in place is essential. Without it, your family may experience significant challenges when attempting to manage your affairs. The Power of Attorney allows you to designate a trusted individual, known as your agent or attorney-in-fact, who can step in and make important decisions on your behalf. This person can pay bills, manage investments, and sell property, ensuring that your family's financial stability and well-being are maintained.

Many adults with children mistakenly believe that their spouse or close family members automatically have the legal authority to make decisions on their behalf. However, this is not the case. Without a Power of Attorney., your loved ones may face unnecessary delays and complications when trying to access your assets or handle your affairs. In some situations, they may even be required to go through a lengthy and expensive legal process to establish guardianship, which can be emotionally and financially draining.

By understanding the importance of a Power of Attorney, you can take proactive steps to protect your family's future. This legal document provides peace of mind, knowing that your wishes will be respected and your loved ones will be empowered to act on your behalf when necessary. It is a crucial component of a comprehensive Texas Estate Planning strategy and can help avoid unnecessary probate proceedings such as a Guardianship proceeding.

Secure Your Legacy: A Comprehensive Guide to Texas Estate Planning serves as an invaluable resource for those putting seeking to educate themselves about putting together an estate plan. It provides step-by-step guidance on creating a Power of Attorney, along with other essential estate planning documents. By utilizing the knowledge and tools provided in this book, readers can navigate the complex world of Texas estate planning and ensure that their loved ones are well taken care of in any circumstances.

In conclusion, understanding the importance of a Power of Attorney is vital. This legal document empowers your chosen agent to make decisions on your behalf, ensuring that your wishes are respected, and your family's well-being is protected. By taking proactive steps and utilizing the guidance provided in this guide you can take your next step towards either preparing an estate plan or updating your existing one.

Appointing an Agent for your Durable Power of Attorney

While one likes to say they have their affairs in order it is really easy to put off estate planning as a person has to deal with their own mortality. However, life can be unpredictable, and unforeseen circumstances may arise where we may not be able to make decisions for ourselves or our loved ones. That is why it is crucial to have a plan in place, such as appointing specific people as your agent on your durable power of attorney, to ensure that things run smoothly even if you become incapacitated.

Selecting and appointing an agent for your power of attorney is an essential part of estate planning. Your power of attorney is a legal document that grants someone you trust, known as the agent or attorney-in-fact, the authority to make decisions on your behalf if you become incapacitated or unable to make decisions for yourself. The powers granted can include financial, legal, among other things.

When it comes to choosing an agent for your durable power of attorney, it is crucial to select someone who is responsible, trustworthy, and understands your values and wishes. This person should be someone you have complete confidence in, as they will be making decisions that directly impact your well-being and financial security.

In Texas, the power of attorney must use the word " durable" to continue in effect once you are incapacitated, meaning it remains effective even if you become incapacitated. Most estate planning attorneys typically use a Durable power of attorney, but some lay people inadvertently prepare a general power of attorney and then the family discovers it terminates once the principal is incapacitated.

Once you have chosen your agent, it is essential to discuss your wishes and expectations with them. Communication is key, as it allows your agent to fully understand your desires regarding your children's upbringing, education, and any other specific instructions you may have. This discussion will ensure that your agent is well-prepared to make decisions that align with your values and wishes. If one is married, I typically advise clients to name their spouse as the first agent and then name 1-3 successor agents. These could be adult children or trusted friends. If you name a few extra then in the event your spouse or the first named agent dies or becomes unable to serve you are still covered by one of the named successor agents. This will prevent your documents from needing to be revised by your estate planning attorney for several years if things work out as expected. This is another reason to review these documents anytime you have a major family event or the dynamics change related to your named agents.

It is important to note that the durable power of attorney must be executed according to the legal requirements in Texas. This includes having the document signed in the presence of a notary public. Failing to meet these requirements may render the power of attorney invalid, which can create unnecessary complications and uncertainties during critical times. You should retain the original because it may need to be recorded with the County Clerk in the event your agent needs to use it to sell real property. Feel free to make copies and provide them to institutions or other third parties that need them, but retain the original just in case you need to record it.

By preparing a durable power of attorney in Texas and naming a few agents, you are taking a proactive step toward securing your family's future. It provides peace of mind, knowing that someone you trust will be able to make important decisions on your behalf, ensuring your family's well-being and financial security are protected.

Advance Directives: Healthcare Directives and Medical Powers of Attorney

When it comes to estate planning, it's crucial to not only consider the distribution of your assets but also plan for future medical decisions. As adults with children, it's essential to ensure that your wishes regarding medical treatments and end-of-life care are known and respected. In Texas, there are two primary tools that can help you achieve this peace of mind: a Healthcare Directive and a Medical Power of Attorney.

A healthcare directive is a legal document that allows you to specify the types of medical treatments you wish to receive or refuse in case you become incapacitated and unable to communicate your preferences. This document allows you to retain control over your medical decisions, even when you are no longer able to express them.

By clearly stating your preferences regarding life-sustaining treatments, such as resuscitation, mechanical ventilation, and artificial nutrition, you can save your loved ones from the emotional burden of making difficult decisions on your behalf.

However, it's essential to understand that a healthcare directive will not cover every medical decision that may arise. That's where a medical power of attorney comes into play. A medical power of attorney is a document that designates a trusted individual, known as your healthcare agent or proxy, to make medical decisions on your behalf if you are unable to do so. The difference between this and the Statutory Durable Power of Attorney that I typically draft is it becomes effective immediately, while your Medical Power of

Attorney only comes alive when you can no longer communicate your healthcare decisions. Also, if you complete the healthcare directive your agent must comply with you designated medical decisions consistent with your healthcare directive.

In this subchapter, we dive deeper into the intricacies of both healthcare directives and medical powers of attorney. We guide you through the process of creating these documents, ensuring that you understand the legal requirements and considerations specific to Texas. We also provide examples and templates to make the process easier for you.

By taking the time to understand and establish these advance directives, you can have peace of mind knowing that your healthcare wishes will be respected, even in the most challenging circumstances.

Communicating Your Healthcare Wishes

Have you considered what would happen if you were unable to make decisions about your own healthcare?

In this subchapter, we will explore the crucial topic of communicating your healthcare wishes. This is another typical document that is addressed when doing your estate planning.

Medical emergencies and unforeseen circumstances can occur at any time, leaving you unable to express your desires regarding medical treatment. This is where advanced healthcare directives and medical power of attorney documents come into play. These legal documents allow you to communicate your healthcare preferences and appoint someone you trust to make medical decisions on your behalf.

Your Healthcare directive outlines your preferences for end-of-life care, such as whether you wish to be kept alive through artificial means or if you prefer a more natural approach. It provides guidance to your family and medical professionals, ensuring your wishes are respected even if you cannot communicate them yourself.

Another vital document is a Medical Power of Attorney. This allows you to appoint a trusted individual to make medical decisions for you if you become incapacitated. It is crucial to choose someone who understands your values and will advocate for your best interests.

When communicating your healthcare wishes, it is essential to have open and honest conversations with your loved ones. Discuss your values, beliefs, and desires regarding medical treatment. This will help them understand your wishes and ensure they can make informed decisions on your behalf. It is very important to not only put this in writing, but also communicate it with all of your closest family members and/or friends so that once the event occurs, they will know you not only told them but also put it in writing. This will greatly improve the odds that the healthcare providers comply with your wishes.

Additionally, it is important to keep your healthcare directives up to date. Life circumstances change, and so do our healthcare preferences. Review your documents periodically, especially after significant life events such as the birth of a child, a divorce, or the loss of a loved one.

By communicating your healthcare wishes and establishing healthcare directives, you are taking proactive steps to secure your legacy and protect your loved ones. Remember, these documents are not just for the elderly or terminally ill; they are for all adults who want to ensure their healthcare preferences are honored.

Chapter 6: Texas Estate Taxes and Probate Avoidance

Overview of Estate Taxes in Texas

When it comes to estate planning in Texas, understanding estate taxes is crucial. Estate taxes refer to the taxes imposed on the transfer of property after an individual's death. Whether you are just beginning your estate planning journey or have already started, having a comprehensive understanding of estate taxes in Texas is essential to ensure the financial security of your loved ones.

In Texas, the good news is that there is currently no state-level estate tax. This means that the state of Texas does not impose its own tax on the transfer of property upon death. However, it's important to note that federal estate taxes may still apply.

The federal estate tax is a tax imposed on the transfer of property at death. For individuals with significant assets, this tax can have a significant impact on the overall value of their estate. However, it's important to understand that federal estate taxes only apply if the value of the estate exceeds the federal estate tax exemption.

As of 2023, the federal estate tax exemption stands at a substantial $ 12.9 million per individual or $25.8 million for a married couple. This means that if the total value of your estate is below these exemption amounts, you won't owe any federal estate taxes. The current exemption is set to go back to old limits in 2025 unless Congress takes action. If they don't then the exemption will drop back to $7 million per individual and $14 million for a couple.

For individuals or couples with estates that exceed the federal estate tax exemption, it's crucial to consider estate planning strategies to minimize or eliminate estate taxes. Some common strategies include gifting assets during your lifetime, creating trusts, and taking advantage of the marital deduction.

It's important to work closely with an experienced estate planning attorney who specializes in Texas estate planning to ensure that your estate plan is tailored to your specific needs and goals.

In conclusion, while Texas does not impose a state-level estate tax, federal estate taxes may still apply. Understanding the federal estate tax exemption and employing effective estate planning strategies can help you minimize or eliminate estate taxes. By proactively planning your estate, you can secure your legacy and provide financial peace of mind for your loved ones.

Strategies to Minimize Estate Taxes in Texas

When it comes to estate planning in Texas, minimizing estate taxes is a crucial consideration for those that happen to have generated wealth in excess of the current federal exemptions. Its also wise to recognize that congress can change that at any point so for high wealth individuals its better to setup a plan for the future that envisions the worst. Most any plan even if you setup an irrevocable trust has a means to provide value to either you or your loved ones even if in the future the estate tax is totally ended.

Though I seek to be non political, I simply can find it in myself to justify someone being taxed on money they earned that was already taxed. I think if Warren Buffet and Bill Gates want to write a check to the Internal Revenue Service for their entire net worth or gift it to them when they die they already have that option.

By understanding and implementing effective strategies, you can ensure that your hard-earned assets are protected and your loved ones are well taken care of. This subchapter will delve into various strategies to minimize estate taxes in the Lone Star State, providing useful insights for those interested in Texas estate planning and probate avoidance.

One of the most common strategies to minimize estate taxes is establishing a trust. By transferring your assets into a trust, you can potentially reduce your estate tax liability. There are several types of trusts available in Texas, each with its own unique advantages. For instance, a revocable living trust allows you to maintain control over your assets during your lifetime while avoiding probate upon your passing. Due note that a typical revocable trust does not provide for tax minimization or asset protection like an irrevocable trust. But it also is a great means for most people with a net worth of $200K - $5M to easily avoid probate and provide a seamless transfer to their family.

On the other hand, an irrevocable trust can provide additional tax benefits, as the assets are no longer considered part of your taxable estate, but then the irrevocable trust has to apply for a tax identification number with the IRS and file its own yearly tax return.

Another effective strategy is making annual gifts to your children or other beneficiaries. Under current tax laws, you can gift up to a certain amount, known as the annual exclusion, without incurring gift taxes. By taking advantage of this exclusion, you can gradually transfer your assets to your loved ones over time, reducing the overall value of your taxable estate. This

Additionally, utilizing the marital deduction can help minimize estate taxes for married couples. In Texas, spouses can leave an unlimited amount of assets to one another without triggering estate taxes. This allows for the preservation of the family wealth and deferral of estate tax until the second spouse passes away.

Charitable giving is yet another strategy that can both benefit your community and reduce estate taxes. By leaving a portion of your assets to qualified charitable organizations, you can lower the taxable value of your estate. This can be especially advantageous when combined with other estate planning strategies.

In conclusion, minimizing estate taxes is a critical goal as you prepare an estate plan. By implementing strategies such as establishing trusts, making annual gifts, utilizing the marital deduction, and engaging in charitable giving, you can protect your assets and ensure a smooth transfer of wealth to your loved ones. It is advisable to consult with an experienced estate planning attorney to tailor these strategies to your specific needs and goals.

Probate Process in Texas: A Comprehensive Guide

It is important to recognize that if you own property in Texas once you die your estate will go to probate, understanding the probate process is crucial for effective estate planning and probate avoidance. This subchapter will provide you with a comprehensive guide to navigating the probate process in Texas, ensuring that your assets are distributed according to your wishes while minimizing the burden on your loved ones.

Probate is the legal process by which a deceased person's assets are transferred to their beneficiaries or heirs. You may or may not find it interesting that Probate dates back to the year 1066 in England. As you may be aware the bulk of United States laws are based on English common law and that's where probate came to be in the United States. In Texas, the probate process can be complex, but with proper planning, it can be streamlined to ensure a smooth transition of your estate.

Probate has been said to be "a lawsuit you start against yourself with your own money for the benefit of your creditors." Not only can probate costs be substantial, but they are also the first to be paid. In many states, the fees are often taken as a percentage of the gross value of the estate (that is, before creditors put a hand in). Here in Texas the fees for probate include court filing, notice fees, and attorney fees typically billed as a flat fee if no one objects and if someone objects then billed by the hour at $350-$750 per hour depending on the attorney and experience

The first step in the probate process is to determine whether the deceased person had a valid will. If a will exists, it must be filed with the appropriate court within four years of the person's death. The court will then appoint an executor, named in the will, to administer the estate. If there is no will, the court will appoint an administrator to handle the estate. If there is no will then in Texas the court is required to appoint an attorney ad litem. His or her job is to investigate all heirs named by the applicant and also search for any potential heirs that were not named. The fees for the attorney ad litem will be paid by the estate and for a simple case will typically range from $750-$1,250 that your estate pays when you don't have a will.

Once appointed, the executor or administrator will gather and inventory the deceased person's assets, pay any outstanding debts or taxes, and distribute the remaining assets to the beneficiaries or heirs. This process can take several months or even years, depending on the complexity of the estate.

However, it is important to note that not all assets are subject to probate. By utilizing various estate planning tools, such as trusts, transfer on death deeds, payable-on-death accounts, and beneficiary designations, along with confirming title to bank accounts is held as Jointly Owned With Rights of Survivorship (JTWROS) you can ensure that certain assets bypass the probate process altogether. This can save time, reduce costs, and maintain privacy for your loved ones. In certain cases, a well-planned estate that is not that complex can totally avoid probate by using the above tools.

To successfully navigate the probate process in Texas, it is essential to consult with an experienced estate planning attorney. They can guide you through the complexities of Texas probate law, help you create a comprehensive estate plan, and assist in probate avoidance strategies.

In conclusion, understanding the probate process in Texas is essential to secure your legacy and minimize the burden on your loved ones. By familiarizing yourself with the probate process and implementing effective estate planning strategies, you can ensure that your assets are distributed according to your wishes and avoid unnecessary delays and expenses. Seek the guidance of an experienced estate planning attorney to navigate this complex process and secure your legacy for future generations.

Tips for Avoiding Probate in Texas

When it comes to estate planning, probate can be a time-consuming and expensive process that can potentially disrupt the distribution of your assets after passing away. Fortunately, there are several strategies you can employ to minimize the probate process in Texas and ensure a smooth transition of your estate to your loved ones.

1. Establish a Revocable Living Trust: Creating a revocable living trust allows you to transfer ownership of your assets to the trust, effectively removing them from your probate estate. This trust allows you to maintain control over your assets during your lifetime while providing a seamless transfer to your beneficiaries upon your passing.

2. Designate Beneficiaries: Many assets, such as life insurance policies, retirement accounts, and investment accounts, allow you to name beneficiaries directly. By designating beneficiaries, these assets will pass outside of probate and directly to your chosen individuals, saving time and potentially avoiding estate taxes.

3. Joint Ownership: Consider joint ownership with rights of survivorship for certain assets such as bank accounts, or vehicles. When one owner passes away, the surviving owner automatically assumes full ownership without the need for probate. The Texas DMV provides a fairly simple form to transfer ownership of a vehicle to the entitled beneficiaries. This is effective for a simple

estate where the children are all children of the Decedent and his/her spouse. If there are children that were born in a previous relationship not part of the current marriage then this may fail.

4. Utilize Payable-on-Death (POD) and Transfer-on-Death (TOD) Designations: For bank accounts and securities, you can name payable-on-death or transfer-on-death beneficiaries. This designation ensures that the assets will transfer directly to the named beneficiaries upon your death, bypassing probate.

5. Gifting: Consider gifting assets to your loved ones during your lifetime. By reducing the size of your estate, you can potentially minimize the probate process and any associated taxes. However, consult with an estate planning attorney to understand the potential gift tax implications.

6. Keep Your Estate Plan Updated: Regularly review and update your estate plan to reflect any changes in your family situation, such as births, deaths, marriages, or divorces. By keeping your plan current, you can ensure that your assets are distributed according to your wishes and streamline the probate process.

Remember, every individual's estate planning needs are unique, so it is essential to consult with an experienced estate planning attorney in Texas to develop a personalized strategy that aligns with your specific circumstances and goals. By taking proactive steps to avoid probate, you can secure your legacy and provide your loved ones with a seamless transition of your assets while minimizing unnecessary costs and stress.

Chapter 7: Protecting Your Legacy and Assets

Essential Asset Protection Strategies in Texas

When it comes to protecting your assets and securing your legacy, it is crucial to have a comprehensive understanding of estate planning and probate avoidance strategies. This subchapter aims to educate you as to essential asset protection strategies to ensure their hard-earned wealth is safeguarded for future generations.

1. Trust-Based Estate Planning: One of the most effective strategies for asset protection is establishing a trust. By creating a revocable living trust, you can transfer your assets into the trust, thereby avoiding probate and ensuring privacy. This allows for the seamless distribution of assets to your children while protecting them from potential creditors or divorce settlements. Do note that there are limitations on how effective a revocable living trust will be in actually avoiding your creditors. A revocable living trust can be set up so that all gifts to children after your death can be protected from bankruptcy, lawsuits, and divorces.

Since you own and control the assets in a revocable living trust creditors can reach it, but you have an extra layer of privacy to help avoid the prying eyes of collection attorneys. The irrevocable trust is more effective in full protection of assets by not allowing a creditor to reach the assets, but you give up most of your control since to be effective you need to name a trustee other than yourself and you have limited options in modifying or revising an irrevocable trust.

2. Homestead Protection: In Texas, the homestead exemption provides significant protection for your primary residence from creditors. Understanding the intricacies of this exemption and filing the necessary paperwork can help safeguard your home from potential claims, providing a secure shelter for your family. Texas is one of only two states that provide an unlimited homestead exemption. This means that if you own a paid off home valued at $10 million and someone sues you and wins they can never get to your home.

3. Business Entity Formation: If you own a business, establishing the right business entity, such as a limited liability company (LLC) or corporation, can shield your personal assets from business-related liabilities. This separation ensures that your personal wealth remains protected in the event of a lawsuit or bankruptcy. Do advise your estate planning attorney of any such business as there is some formation and/or operating agreements that may need to be put in place to effectively deal with you passing away. If it is a closely held LLC with say 3 members then you may want an agreement in place that if any of the three die the others can buy out that member's interest within a certain period of time.

4. Insurance Coverage: Proper insurance coverage is essential to protect your assets from unforeseen events. Reviewing your policies regularly and ensuring they adequately cover potential risks can provide financial security to your family. Additionally, umbrella insurance policies can offer an extra layer of protection, covering any liability that exceeds the limits of your other policies.

5. Marital Property Agreements: For married couples, entering into a prenuptial or postnuptial agreement can establish guidelines for asset

division in the event of divorce or death. These agreements can protect individual assets and prevent disputes, ensuring a smooth transition for your children.

6. Family Limited Partnerships (FLPs): FLPs enable you to transfer assets to family members while retaining control. By gifting limited partnership interests, you can decrease your taxable estate and protect your assets from potential creditors or lawsuits.

It is important to consult with an experienced estate planning attorney in Texas to understand these strategies fully and tailor them to your unique circumstances. By implementing these essential asset protection strategies, you can secure your legacy and provide a solid foundation for your families future financial well-being.

Homestead Exemption and Protection

One of the key considerations in Texas estate planning is understanding the Homestead Exemption and Protection laws. This subchapter aims to provide adults with children an in-depth understanding of how this exemption works and how it can help protect their family's assets. Whether you already own a home or plan to in the future, knowing the ins and outs of this provision is crucial to ensuring the security of your legacy.

The Homestead Exemption is a legal provision that provides certain protections for homeowners against creditors. In Texas, the homestead is defined as the place of residence for an individual or family. It can be a house, condo, or even a mobile home, as long as it serves as the primary residence. The exemption allows homeowners to shield all of their equity in their homestead from being seized by creditors or used to satisfy debts. This protection is especially vital for families who wish to pass down their home to their children.

In Texas, the homestead exemption is automatic, meaning it is applied by law without the need for any formal declaration or filing. However, there are limitations to the amount of equity that can be protected, primarily if you file bankruptcy otherwise your exemption is unlimited.

To fully maximize the benefits of the homestead exemption, it is crucial to understand the intricacies of Texas homestead laws. For instance, if you plan to sell your current homestead and purchase a new one, there are specific rules and timeframes that must be followed to retain the exemption on the proceeds from the sale. Additionally, if you are married, both spouses must join in the homestead designation to ensure that full protection is available.

By taking advantage of the Homestead Exemption and Protection laws, Texas residents can safeguard their family's most valuable asset – their home. Understanding the limits and requirements of this provision is vital for effective estate planning and probate avoidance. With proper planning, you can ensure that your children inherit a secure and debt-free home, preserving your legacy for generations to come.

Insurance Considerations for Estate Planning in Texas

When it comes to estate planning in Texas, there are several important insurance considerations that you may want to take into account. Insurance can play a crucial role in protecting your assets and ensuring that your loved ones are taken care of in the event of your passing. In this subchapter, we will explore the various insurance options available and how they can be integrated into your estate plan to provide maximum protection for your family.

One of the key insurance considerations is life insurance. Life insurance policies can provide a source of income for your beneficiaries, helping to cover expenses such as mortgage payments, education costs, and daily living expenses. It can also be used to pay off debts or estate taxes, ensuring that your loved ones are not burdened with financial obligations. We will discuss the different types of life insurance policies available, such as term and whole life insurance, and help you determine the right coverage amount based on your specific circumstances.

Another important insurance consideration is long-term care insurance. As you age, the need for long-term care services may arise, whether it be in-home care, assisted living, or a nursing home. Long-term care insurance can help cover these expenses, which can be substantial and quickly deplete your savings. We will explore the benefits of long-term care insurance and help you determine if it is a suitable option for your estate plan.

Additionally, we will discuss disability insurance, which can provide income replacement in the event of a disabling injury or illness that prevents you from working. Disability insurance can help protect your family's financial stability and ensure that your estate plan remains intact even if you are unable to generate income.

Finally, we will touch on liability insurance, which is often overlooked in estate planning discussions. Liability insurance can protect your assets in the event that you are sued for damages or injuries caused by you or your property. By having adequate liability coverage, you can shield your estate from potential lawsuits and preserve your assets for future generations.

In conclusion, insurance considerations are an integral part of estate planning in Texas. By understanding the various insurance options available and how they can be integrated into your estate plan, you can ensure that your loved ones are protected and your assets are preserved.

Legacy Planning: Charitable Giving and Philanthropy

We understand the importance of leaving a lasting legacy for future generations. Legacy planning goes beyond simply passing on our assets and wealth to our loved ones. It involves making a positive impact on our communities and the world through charitable giving and philanthropy. In this subchapter, we will explore the significance of incorporating charitable giving into your Texas estate planning and how it can help you create a meaningful legacy.

Charitable giving is an opportunity to support causes that are close to your heart and make a difference in the lives of others. By including charitable donations in your estate plan, you can ensure that your values and passions continue to be upheld long after you are gone. Whether it's supporting education, healthcare, environmental conservation, or any other cause, your philanthropic efforts can leave a lasting impact on the world around you.

By integrating charitable giving into your estate plan, you can also enjoy certain tax benefits. Charitable contributions can reduce the size of your taxable estate, potentially lowering estate taxes for your heirs. Additionally, creating a charitable foundation or trust can provide ongoing support to your chosen causes, while allowing you to retain control over how your funds are used.

When considering charitable giving as part of your legacy plan, it is essential to identify your philanthropic goals and values. Reflect on the causes that resonate with you and align with your family's values. Engage your children in conversations about charitable giving, encouraging them to develop their own philanthropic interests. By involving your family in these decisions, you can instill a sense of purpose and responsibility in the next generation.

Furthermore, it is crucial to work with an experienced estate planning attorney who specializes in estate planning. They will guide you through the process of structuring your charitable giving strategies, ensuring compliance with all legal requirements and maximizing the impact of your philanthropic efforts.

In conclusion, legacy planning is about more than just preserving your wealth for future generations. It is an opportunity to create a lasting impact on the causes and communities you care about. By integrating charitable giving and philanthropy into your Texas estate planning, you can leave a meaningful legacy that continues to make a difference long after you are gone. Start planning your legacy today and ensure that your values endure for generations to come.

Chapter 8: Special Considerations for Adult Children

Navigating Family Dynamics in Estate Planning

When it comes to estate planning, it's important to consider not only the legal and financial aspects but also the dynamics within your family. Estate planning is not just about distributing assets; it's about ensuring that your loved ones are taken care of and minimizing conflicts that may arise after you're gone. In this subchapter, we will explore the unique challenges that adults with children face in estate planning and how to navigate family dynamics to secure your legacy in Texas.

One of the first considerations is ensuring that your wishes are clearly communicated to your family. Open and honest communication is key to avoiding misunderstandings and potential disputes. It's important to discuss your estate plan with your children and other family members, explaining your intentions and reasoning behind certain decisions. By involving them in the process, you can help them understand your choices and minimize any potential conflicts. There are certain situations where discussing all of this could cause more conflict. Discuss this with you attorney and he or she may be able to either help minimize conflict or discuss how best to address it.

It's also crucial to understand the unique dynamics within your family. Each family is different, and there may be existing tensions or conflicts that need to be addressed. For example, if you have a blended family, you may need to take extra precautions to ensure fair treatment of all children and stepchildren. By addressing these dynamics head-on and seeking professional advice, you can design an estate plan that takes into account the specific needs and circumstances of your family.

Choosing the right executor or trustee is another important aspect of estate planning that can impact family dynamics. It's essential to select someone who is not only trustworthy and capable but also neutral and impartial. This can help alleviate potential conflicts among family members and ensure that your wishes are carried out effectively.

In addressing these conflicts don't forget that you should probably consult with an estate planning attorney and explain your goals and objectives as they have probably seen every variation of planning options. In doing this, they may be able to address your concerns and come up with a plan that helps diminish the conflict.

In conclusion, estate planning is not just about the legal and financial aspects; it also involves understanding and navigating the dynamics within your family. By openly communicating with your loved ones, addressing unique family dynamics, choosing the right executor, and seeking professional advice, you can secure your legacy and minimize conflicts after you're gone. Remember, estate planning is not a one-time event but an ongoing process that should be reviewed and updated regularly to reflect any changes in your family or financial situation. Do note that in the end, it is up to you. You have the right to give your estate to whomever you choose and it is your attorney's job to make sure that is accomplished. There is no need to go into long detail about why you want one child to receive nothing.

I generally just want to know how likely they are to challenge a will or question a trust and once I know that I will develop a written plan that accomplishes the clients' goal.

Planning for Special Needs Children and Dependents

When it comes to estate planning, it is crucial to consider the needs of your special needs children and dependents. Special needs individuals require extra care and attention, both during your lifetime and after you are gone. Take proactive steps to secure their future and ensure they receive the support they need. In this subchapter, we will explore the key aspects of planning for special needs children and dependents within the context of estate planning.

First and foremost, it is essential to establish a comprehensive special needs plan. This includes identifying the unique requirements and challenges your special needs child or dependent may face throughout their life. By understanding their specific needs, you can create a tailored plan that addresses their financial, medical, and emotional well-being.

One critical element of special needs planning is the creation of a Supplemental Needs Trust (SNT). A properly drafted SNT allows you to set aside funds for your special needs child or dependent without jeopardizing their eligibility for government benefits such as Medicaid and Supplemental Security Income (SSI). By utilizing an SNT, you can ensure that your child's quality of life remains intact even after your passing. An SNT does have special requirements related to what the trust can pay for and what it can not. Generally, anything within a broad list of items can be purchased to help them have a better standard of living. This could be something as simple as a TV and game system updated yearly for an autistic child knowing that this an area that betters their daily life.

Additionally, it is imperative to appoint a guardian for your special needs child or dependent. This individual will be responsible for making important decisions regarding their care, finances, and medical treatment. Selecting the right guardian is crucial, as they will play a significant role in safeguarding your child's well-being and ensuring their best interests are always prioritized.

Furthermore, it is essential to update your estate plan regularly. As your special needs child or dependent grows and their circumstances change, it is crucial to adjust your plan accordingly.

Lastly, it is advisable to seek professional guidance from an experienced Texas estate planning attorney. They can provide valuable insights and expertise in navigating the complexities of special needs planning. An attorney can help you understand the legal requirements, assist in creating a comprehensive plan, and ensure your wishes are effectively documented and legally binding.

By taking these proactive steps and addressing the unique needs of your special needs children and dependents, you can secure their future and provide them with the support they require. Planning for special needs individuals requires careful consideration, but with the right guidance, you can ensure your legacy is preserved and your loved ones are protected.

Estate Planning for Blended Families in Texas

We understand the importance of planning for the future. Estate planning is a crucial step to ensure that our loved ones are taken care of after we are gone. However, for blended families in Texas, estate planning can become more complex due to the unique dynamics involved. In this subchapter, we will explore the intricacies of estate planning for blended families in Texas and provide guidance on how to navigate these challenges.

Blended families, consisting of couples who have children from previous relationships, require careful consideration when it comes to estate planning. One of the key concerns is determining how to distribute assets between the spouse and children from previous relationships. Without proper planning, conflicts and disputes may arise, potentially jeopardizing family relationships and causing unnecessary stress during an already difficult time.

In Texas, estate planning for blended families typically involves the use of various legal instruments, such as wills, trusts, and prenuptial agreements. These tools can help ensure that your assets are distributed according to your wishes, provide for your current spouse, and protect the interests of your children from previous relationships.

One popular option is the creation of a trust. By establishing a trust, you can control the distribution of your assets, specify how and when your beneficiaries will receive their inheritance, and provide for your surviving spouse while still protecting your children's interests. Trusts can be particularly useful in situations where there is a significant age difference between spouses or when a surviving spouse remarries.

In conclusion, estate planning for blended families in Texas requires careful consideration and the use of appropriate legal instruments. By working with an experienced estate planning attorney, you can develop a comprehensive plan that addresses the unique needs of your blended family. Secure Your Legacy:

Discussing Your Estate Plan with Adult Children

One of the most important aspects of estate planning is ensuring that your wishes are communicated effectively to your loved ones, especially your adult children. While it may be a sensitive and challenging topic to broach, discussing your estate plan with your adult children is essential to avoid confusion, conflicts, and potential legal issues after your passing. In this subchapter, we will delve into the significance of having open and honest conversations with your adult children about your estate plan, specifically tailored to the context of Texas.

When it comes to estate planning, transparency is key. Adult children should be aware of the decisions you have made regarding your assets, property, and final wishes. This will not only provide them with a sense of security but also allow them to understand and respect your choices. A well-structured estate plan can help avoid disputes and misunderstandings among your beneficiaries, ensuring a smooth transition of your estate.

Estate planning can be complex due to the specific laws and regulations that govern this area. Therefore, it is crucial to involve your adult children in the process, especially if you have appointed them as executors or trustees. Discussing the responsibilities, duties, and potential challenges they may face will help them prepare and make informed decisions when the time comes.

Moreover, involving your adult children in your estate planning can provide an opportunity to educate them about the importance of having their own estate plans. This conversation can serve as a catalyst for them to start planning for their future and ensure that their loved ones are protected.

To effectively discuss your estate plan with your adult children, it is essential to choose the right time and place. Create a comfortable and private environment where everyone can express their thoughts and concerns openly. Be patient, understanding, and empathetic, as your adult children may have their own emotions and apprehensions about the topic.

Remember, estate planning is not a one-time conversation. As your circumstances and wishes evolve over time, it is crucial to periodically update your adult children about any changes or additions to your estate plan. This ongoing dialogue will help maintain clarity and prevent any potential surprises or misunderstandings in the future.

In conclusion, discussing your estate plan with your adult children is a vital step in securing your legacy and ensuring a seamless transition of assets. By involving them in the process and fostering open communication, you can provide them with a sense of security.

I recognize that the dynamics in certain families does not allow for this discussion due to unresolved conflict, etc. As an estate planning attorney I like to better understand the family dynamics with my clients and then discuss with them if they should potentially avoid the discussion other than telling them where to find the documents and talking these issues over with the named executor to Will or successor trustee on their trust.

Chapter 9: Reviewing and Updating Your Estate Plan

Importance of Regularly Reviewing Your Estate Plan

We work hard to provide for our loved ones and ensure their well-being even after we are no longer around. That is why having a comprehensive estate plan is crucial. Regularly reviewing your estate plan is an essential step in ensuring that your wishes are accurately reflected and that your loved ones are protected.

There are several reasons why reviewing your estate plan is so important. Firstly, life is dynamic, and circumstances change. You may experience significant life events such as marriage, divorce, birth of a child, or the death of a loved one. These events can impact your estate planning needs and require adjustments to your plan. Regularly reviewing your estate plan allows you to ensure that it accurately reflects your current wishes and protects the best interests of your children.

Secondly, tax laws and regulations are subject to change, and these changes can have a significant impact on your estate plan. By staying informed and working with an experienced estate planning attorney, you can ensure that your plan remains tax-efficient and minimizes potential tax burdens for your loved ones.

Additionally, regularly reviewing your estate plan gives you the opportunity to evaluate the appointed individuals in crucial roles such as guardians for minor children, trustees, or executors. People's circumstances and relationships change, and it is important to ensure that the right individuals are entrusted with these responsibilities.

In conclusion, regularly reviewing your estate plan is a vital aspect of estate planning. Life is dynamic, and circumstances change, necessitating adjustments to your plan. By staying informed, staying up to date with changes in laws and regulations, and working with an experienced estate planning attorney, you can ensure that your plan accurately reflects your wishes and provides for the well-being of your children and loved ones. Take the time to review your estate plan regularly – it is an investment in securing your legacy and providing peace of mind.

Life Events and Circumstances That Require Plan Updates

It is crucial to remember that estate planning is not a one-time task. Life is full of unexpected twists and turns, and certain life events and circumstances may require updates to your existing estate plan. In this subchapter, we will explore some of these significant life events and circumstances that necessitate plan updates, specifically in the context of Texas estate planning and probate avoidance.

Firstly, as our children grow older, their needs and circumstances change. This includes milestones such as turning 18, graduating from college, getting married, or having children of their own. Each of these events may impact the distribution of your assets and the individuals you designate as beneficiaries or fiduciaries in your estate plan. Regularly reviewing and updating your plan ensures that it aligns with your current wishes and the needs of your children.

Secondly, changes in your financial situation may require plan updates. This could include significant increases or decreases in assets, changes in business ownership, or acquiring new properties or investments. By revisiting your estate plan, you can make necessary adjustments to ensure that your assets are properly protected and distributed according to your wishes.

Additionally, changes in relationships and family dynamics may necessitate plan updates. Divorce, remarriage, or the death of a spouse may impact your intended beneficiaries, guardians for minor children, or even the individuals you have named as executors or trustees. Keeping your estate plan up to date ensures that these important decisions accurately reflect your current circumstances.

Furthermore, changes in state or federal laws can significantly impact your estate plan. Estate planning and probate laws are subject to change, and it is essential to stay informed about any revisions that may affect your plan. By working with an experienced estate planning attorney, you can ensure that your plan is always in compliance with the latest legal requirements.

In conclusion, estate planning is an ongoing process that requires periodic updates to reflect changes in life events, circumstances, and laws. By staying proactive and regularly reviewing your plan, you can secure your legacy and provide peace of mind for yourself and your loved ones. Remember, it is never too late to make updates and adjustments to your estate plan to ensure that it remains relevant and effective throughout your life.

Seeking Professional Guidance for Plan Updates

As the saying goes, change is the only constant in life. This holds true when it comes to your estate planning as well. Life events such as the birth of a child, acquiring significant assets, or changes in marital status can all impact the effectiveness of your estate plan. That is why seeking professional guidance for plan updates is crucial to ensure your wishes are carried out effectively and your loved ones are protected.

In the realm of estate planning and probate avoidance, it is crucial to understand that laws and regulations can change over time. What may have been a sound strategy a few years ago may no longer be relevant or effective today.

One of the most common life events that prompt plan updates is the birth of a child. With the arrival of a new family member, it becomes essential to address guardianship provisions and ensure your child's well-being in the event of an unexpected tragedy. A skilled attorney can guide you through the process of designating a guardian and updating your will accordingly. If this is anticipated your attorney can simply add that any afterborn children will be treated the same as existing children.

Similarly, acquiring significant assets or experiencing changes in marital status can have a significant impact on your estate plan. Whether it's purchasing real estate, starting a business, or going through a divorce, these events may require adjustments to your plan to protect your assets and ensure they are distributed according to your wishes.

By seeking professional guidance for plan updates, you can also take advantage of new strategies or tools that may have emerged since your original plan was created. For example, there may be new methods for probate avoidance or tax planning that can help preserve your wealth and minimize the burden on your loved ones.

Don't leave your legacy to chance. Seek professional guidance for plan updates to secure your family's future and protect the fruits of your hard work.

Legacy Planning: Leaving a Lasting Impact

In the journey of life, we all strive to leave a lasting impact on the world., We have an even greater responsibility to secure our legacy and ensure that our loved ones are taken care of when we're no longer here. Legacy planning is a crucial part of the estate planning process, and it allows us to create a roadmap for future generations.

Legacy planning is more than just creating a will or a trust. It involves careful consideration of your values, goals, and aspirations, and how you want them reflected in the lives of your children and grandchildren. It's about passing on not just your wealth, but also your wisdom, experiences, and the values that have shaped you.

One of the key aspects of legacy planning is financial planning. It involves assessing your current financial situation and determining how to best preserve and grow your assets for the benefit of your children and future generations. This may include setting up trusts, establishing charitable foundations, or creating educational funds to support your family's goals.

But legacy planning goes beyond finances. It also encompasses your personal and family history, your values, and your wishes for the future. It's about passing on your stories, faith, traditions, and values to the next generation. This can be achieved through the creation of ethical wills or family mission statements, which provide guidance and direction for your loved ones.

An important part of legacy planning is also ensuring that your estate is properly managed and distributed. By engaging in probate avoidance strategies, you can minimize unnecessary taxes, delays, and expenses that can erode your wealth. This may involve utilizing tools such as living trusts, gifting strategies, or beneficiary designations to streamline the transfer of assets.

Moreover, legacy planning allows you to address important end-of-life decisions, such as healthcare directives and powers of attorney. By clearly expressing your wishes, you can ensure that your medical care and financial affairs are handled according to your preferences, relieving your loved ones of the burden of making difficult decisions during emotionally challenging times.

By engaging in legacy planning, you can leave a lasting impact on your family, your community, and the causes you hold dear. It's an opportunity to weave your values and dreams into the fabric of the future, ensuring that your legacy lives on in the hearts and minds of those you love. Start your journey today and secure your legacy for generations to come.

Conclusion: Taking Control of Your Future Through Texas Estate Planning

Planning for the future, especially in terms of estate planning, is crucial to secure your legacy and protect your family's financial future. In this subchapter, we have explored the key elements of Texas Estate Planning and Probate Avoidance, empowering you to take control of your future.

By taking the time to create a comprehensive estate plan, you can ensure that your assets are distributed according to your wishes, minimize the burden of probate on your loved ones, and protect your family's financial security. Texas estate planning offers a variety of tools and strategies to achieve these goals, from wills and trusts to powers of attorney and healthcare directives.

One of the most common misconceptions regarding estate planning is that it is only for the wealthy. However, regardless of your wealth or the size of your estate, estate planning is essential for every adult. It allows you to make informed decisions about guardianship for your minor children, designate beneficiaries for your assets, and even plan for long-term care expenses. For those more senior that have lost their spouse or are alone, they may want to designate a named guardian for themselves and also to identify people they don't want to be named as a guardian.

Remember, estate planning is an ongoing process, and it is essential to periodically review and update your plan to accommodate any changes in your life circumstances.

www.ingramcontent.com/pod-product-compliance
Lightning Source LLC
Chambersburg PA
CBHW062242290526
45794CB00006B/2367